Build Your Business Fast!

ABOUT THE AUTHOR

Tonisha Dawson has been a licensed cosmetologist and aesthetician for fifteen years. She holds advanced and master certificates in Makeup Artistry, Expert Waxing, Barbering, Aromatherapy, Reflexology, Nail Care, Haircutting, Coloring and Holistic Life Coaching. She has since been known as a Master Educator and Teacher in the industry, having taught Cosmetology to students for the past six years. She works as a successful Aesthetician and Makeup Artist as well as a Master Educator certifying students to become Nail Techs, Makeup Artist, Waxing Techs and Aestheticians.

BUILD YOUR BEAUTY BUSINESS FAST!!

How to Network & Build your Clientele in a Timely Manner

By Tonisha L. Dawson

ISBN -13: 978-1507752623

ISBN-10: 1507752628

osunallurebeauty@gmail.com

Disclaimer: The author of this book has put together this work for the purpose of business assistance. The author makes no guarantees or promises of results and will not be held liable for loss or damages. This work does not represent the expert opinion of a business consultant, and if the reader is in need of professional assistance, the author encourages the reader to seek a professional for services needed.

Table of Contents

Introduction

This book will be your go to guide to help you successfully build your beauty business. It does not matter whether you are a Hairdresser, Makeup Artist, Aesthetician, Barber, Consultant, Nail Technician, Expert Waxer, Educator, Salon or Spa Coordinator, Manager or anything in between, the principles in this easy read are universal and if implemented correctly will most assuredly help you to build your business…swiftly.

You may be wondering how I have this information privy to me to share with you, but let me tell you, I have been in this industry over fifteen years and I am still young and going strong. As a young girl I always knew that I wanted a career in the beauty industry, I was obsessed with dolls and makeup and had little interest in anything else besides reading. My grandmother was in cosmetology school while I was a very young girl and I was super intrigued by her coming home studying and bringing home her mannequin heads to practice on. She used to do hair in her home and turned her downstairs area into a fully functioning salon. My mother also dabbled in the industry but she had no interest in pursuing a full time career of it. I remember the smell of acrylic nails as my mother would be doing my aunts nails, or watching her make up other women's faces. I just LOVED the whole idea of it, and I knew that as soon as I became of age, this is what I wanted to do.

A few more years passed and I was now in high school. I gravitated toward a certain group of friends and they were also totally into beauty and looking good. Everyone knew that if you had a makeup emergency or a quick fix up, we were somewhere to be found. I carried tweezers, lip liner, eye liner, a flatiron and little essentials in my bag on a daily basis. I can't even count how many times I got caught on numerous occasions tweezing eyebrows in the lunchroom during break or study hall and at times even flat ironing a friend's hair!

My parents would come to me asking what I wanted to do career wise as I grew up and I had two answers; either I wanted to be a Cosmetologist or an Obstetrician/Gynecologist and seeing as though I was never really great at Math or Science becoming a doctor was far beyond my reach. I also knew that I didn't want to attend school after high school for another 6-8 years. This eliminated my doctor possibility for sure! I ended up entering Cosmetology school at the tender at of 17 with my parent's permission. I went to high school during the day and Cosmetology school at night, it was difficult and I had to work hard but I finally made it! 2 years later I graduated cosmetology school and immediately entered into the Aesthetics Program. This program was also a yearlong and I graduated with flying colors.

Shortly after, I was hired at a very popular salon in my area and before I knew it, I was making loads of money every week! This salon was structured, had a system and was run a certain way. This was my first experience in the salon business and it paved the way for my future. Since that first experience, I have worked in various aspects of the industry. I have worked as a Stylist, Salon Manager, Salon/Spa Coordinator, Makeup Artist, Salon Consultant, Cosmetology Educator and most recently Master Educator and Esthetician where I facilitate my own certifiable course and teach effective salon business courses.

This career has been great and rewarding for me and it can be the same for you! The principles and advice given in this book, will help you to build a clientele timely, keep existing clients, learn how to approach perspective clients, shed light on how you lose clients, and ultimately shows you how to take your business to the next level!

1

<u>ALL ABOUT YOU</u>

This segment is all about you. Why? Because you are your business! In this industry your business is YOU and non-other.

There may be many reasons for why you chose this industry. There are almost too many to name; the flexibility, the pace of it, the constant interaction with people, the excitement of it, showcasing your creativity, and the list goes on and on.

These all great reasons to enter into the beauty industry but they will not sustain your career in this industry. What will sustain your career is, your LOVE of the industry, your PASSION for the industry and your

DESIRE to service others. This is the basis for the Cosmetology industry.

Let's talk about these three things for a moment. Your Love of the industry will keep you satisfied in your career. When you do not love what you do, you are usually not very good at what you do. This industry is constantly growing, moving and changing because the trends are constantly growing, moving and changing. Beauty evolves and there are always new techniques and tricks that come out and keep us on our toes. If you do not truly love what you are doing, continuing education will be a burden for you and not an exciting endeavor. You will lose steam after a couple of years of standing on your feet and dealing with picky clients. Clients can be very demanding and this can be very stressful if you are not built to handle it. The constant changing of the industry might begin to frustrate you and you may find yourself losing interest altogether. There are many things that go on in a salon and spa atmosphere that you may not be a fan of, but if you love what you do, it does not have a big effect on you as you strive to build your business. The love of the business is what keeps you coming to work every day. Most people in the beauty business work weekends and usually do not get a weekend off, unless for vacation. This is a sacrifice that you make as a Cosmo, and love is what will keep you pushing through this. If you are iffy about whether this is the career for you, you will find out relatively quickly as the long hours, weekend days and impeccable customer service will begin to take its toll. I have seen all too many times as an instructor, students come in because their parents made them or because they needed *something* to do after high school. They would immediately lose focus, hate the work that had to be done and ultimately ended up quitting school or shortly after obtaining work, realize this is not the path they should have taken. I have seen students with amazing talent, but preferred to be doing something else entirely.

Passion is key, because this is where your creativity derives from. This industry is all about creativity. It does not matter if you are a Makeup Artist, Body Waxer, Skin Care Specialist or Colorist, you have to find ways to be creative to get around problems and come up with solutions. There are many small things as well as disastrous things that can happen as a result of your line of work and your passion is what will get you through it. There are color catastrophes, allergic reactions to chemicals or skin care, waxing boo boo's, pedicure problems, makeup mix ups, and haircutting hang ups. These are all everyday obstacles that you may have to hurdle over the course of eight hours. This is where the job becomes fun! At times it can be stressful of course, but overall, your creativity is what will propel you forward. Passion helps to keep you up to date. Have you ever seen that hairdresser or makeup artist that seems like they are stuck in the eighties? These people have lost their passion a LONG time ago and left their skills back there as well! This industry moves and shakes, it has forward momentum. What worked last summer is not the look for this summer and you have to be passionate enough to keep up. Classes are given on a consistent basis to help you sharpen your skills and it is wise to stay educated if you are going to be a great cosmetologist. No matter what segment you desire to obtain mastery in, you have to stay abreast with what is current. Passion is talent mixed with love. When you have a talent for something and you also love doing it, it will show in your work and dedication to your craft. Clients will sense this and begin to trust you. Everyone can tell when someone is burnt out or their passion has run thin. Clients have a special knack for this because this is a touch based industry and they can feel the energy of the person working on them and vice versa. They can feel if their servicer is annoyed, tired, burnt out, stressed, or discontented with their job. This will ultimately cause your business to suffer, so you may as well get out while you still have time to pursue another career.

You will have to possess a sincere desire to service others because that is what this industry is all about. This is a *servicing* industry, so you have to like people just a teensy bit to be successful. I am being fastidious, but seriously, you have to have a sincere desire to serve others in order for this industry to work for you. This is of extreme importance because if you do not genuinely like people or being around people, I am here to tell you that you will NOT be successful. It does not matter whether you are the owner and stay tucked away in your office or the shampoo girl who only assists others, if you are not people oriented your business will fail. There are many reasons for this. First and foremost, you are dealing with clients and customers on a daily basis. These clients and customers want your undivided attention and impeccable customer service, they want to feel warm and welcomed when they enter and they don't want to feel unappreciated or dismissed. Let's face it, there are some personalities that are better with people than others. Some people are friendly by nature and also people oriented and not shy. There are others who are shy and very introverted, and even others who would prefer not to be around people at all. The latter two will have a very hard time building a successful beauty business because you have to be able to talk to clients to get them to come see you! I worked with a young woman who was actually not in the industry but was a front desk coordinator. I cannot begin to tell you how many clients were lost as result of her work ethic and attitude. She was promoted to manager to everyone's dismay simply because she was good with computers and marketing, HOWEVER a talent with technology does not make for a good manager. This woman made mountains out of molehills, always found something to complain about, was an avid storyteller, never said good morning to the staff, was not friendly, always angry or annoyed, loved negativity and not to mentioned she always looked as though she had been put in the washing machine on the spin cycle. She came into the business, took over, and the owners who were usually not accessible, began taking her word for everything. Before you knew it, there was a lot of discontentment in the building and disgruntled employees as well as clients. As you can probably predict, there was a massive walkout leaving a business that started with a staff of thirty down to a staff of about twelve. That's a big hit and we all suffered! The actions of just one employee, almost burned an entire business to the ground based on her attitude. This is how important customer service is to this business. Customer service will be your biggest attribute to gaining clients and keeping clients. If you are shy and introverted and possibly afraid to talk or initiate conversation, this may not be the career for you. Although you may have great talent and a love for the business, you will have a hard time gaining clients and keeping clients until you learn to come out of your shell. If you do not have a natural "like" for people, this career will be gut wrenching, as most clients love to talk to you and listen to you talk to them. If you are not a people person, you can still work in the industry, however you may be better off in a position behind the scenes. There are many options that are still available for you if this is the case. You can do hair and makeup at a funeral home where your client is guaranteed not to talk to you, you can be a stylist or makeup artist on a television or movie set where most celebrities do not want to talk anyway, you can be a private consultant and only deal with a few clients on a consistent basis, the possibilities vary and are modifiable based on what you like to do.

Another aspect that is interesting about this industry and will affect your success level in a big way is your love of helping people. You have to enjoy helping people and taking them to another level to be fully functional in this business. When clients come to you, they are coming to you for assistance. They may need a new look, image consulting, skin care techniques, makeup tips and tricks, nail designs, or a hairless body...whatever the cause may be, they are coming to you to bring them to that next level. This aspect alone should be of upmost concern to you. This should give you the high that reveals to you how purposeful your career truly is. You are helping women and men upgrade their image daily. You are a very important pinnacle in their life. Just think of this, the day before someone gets married they come see you, the day before a big event, they come see you, when a job opportunity arises and they have to be interviewed, they come see you! Baby showers, Bridal Showers, Birthday parties, Concerts, First Dates, Divorces, Girls Night, Boys Night, whatever the event, clients come to see YOU!!! This is the part to revel and take heart in. People love to be beautiful and feel good about themselves and you are a big part of that process!

Years ago, the cosmetology industry was not respected and anyone who wanted to go into this particular line of work was considered flighty or better yet, had no promising future doing anything else and was left with this to run forward with. Nowadays cosmetologist are being flown in just to do an impeccable eyebrow job and a quick facial before an interview.

The industry has evolved in so many ways, and is now widely respected as a promising career. There are many avenues you can take as you embark on your exciting new future. You can become a Stylist, Colorist, Educator, Consultant, Sales Rep, Salon/Spa Manager, Salon/Spa Coordinator, Makeup Artist, Aesthetician, Nail Tech, Barber, Platform Artist, Waxing Tech, Stylist Assistant, Weave & Extension Specialist and the list truly goes on and on. The possibilities are very expansive in this industry and you get out of it what you decide to put into it. When you offer love, caring and dedication to your craft, it will produce for you consistent and reliable results as it comes to success with your clients.

The best timing for evaluating if this is the right career for you would be while you are attending school. Although we all disliked hair school as it is commonly called, it does give you a basic picture of what's to come for you. Cosmetology school usually only teaches you the basics of hairstyling, skin and nails, and it is up to you to decide to take continuing education courses once school is completed. This will be easy, as most salons and spas offer education for you to take part in while you are employed at their place of business. This ensures them that you are properly educated as a Stylist or Esthetician while employed. It is also important that you explore many arenas while you are at school. This will help you to sort out what you like to do and what you absolutely detest doing. As a student, I absolutely hated permanent waves. I had to do a select amount of them while being educated, however, once out of school, I don't think I ever touched a permanent wave again! I disliked the smell, I did not like what it did to the integrity of the hair and overall I didn't like the process. Even though I did not partake in doing perms, it did not affect my business one bit, why? Because there is always someone else that will be willing to do them. That is the great thing about this industry, you can be as selective as you please without it impacting your business in a big way.

While in school, ask yourself, do you *love* what you are doing? Do you have passion for it? Do you like interacting with clients and doing the practical segment of the education? If not, you may as well get out now. You will have done nothing but waste time and a significant amount of student loans only to realize that you want to embark down another path for your life. If you realize that you absolutely LOVE what you are doing and have passion for it, then make sure you stick it out. Cosmetology school is not always a picnic and you can lose sight of your original goal while you are there, I've seen it happen myself so many times as an educator. Students will lose heart in the middle of the program or become annoyed at teachers and peers only to quit realizing that they have made a huge mistake.

If you are in school or thinking about attending Cosmetology school or even possibly owning your own business and want to grow it in a fresh way, keep loving it, keep your passion, hold on to your creativity and this will be the catalyst that keeps your career intact for the long haul. Remember, you are your own business whether you work in someone else's business or not. You will be the one who keeps your business afloat or help it to sink, you are the magnet, that will draw clients to you and your energy and creativity is what will keep them with you. This is why it is ALL ABOUT YOU!

2

<u>WHO TO TARGET</u>

When looking to build your business, whether you are fresh out of school or already existing in business, the first question you want to ask is "Who do I target?" the answer to this question is; at first everyone, by the sheer law of numbers you can win clients. So, let's get into how you can begin to target your potential clients.

BUSINESS CARDS

First things first, you have to get cards made. Business cards that is. Business cards give you a professional image and contain all the information needed to guide the client your way. They show that you take pride in your business and that you have taken the time to make it look professional. Business cards are a must have in this industry because as I stated before you are your business and when others see you out and about, it is something physical that you can hand to them. How many times have you gone out and seen someone you know or a friend of a friend and you tell them about your business only to realize that you don't have anything to hand them. They will always tell you that they are coming to get a service, but without something physical to remind them of you, they may forget as soon as they walk away. It is very common for someone to get into a beauty crisis and remember your card in their wallet, they call you during their time of need and you end up with a client for the long haul.

As a fresh student or even a seasoned business builder, you want to pass these cards out every opportunity that arises. I have been told that my shoes were nice and I handed them a business card. I do not waste time to let anyone know that I can help to upgrade their image.

This gives you a chance to spark conversation and anytime anything physical is placed into their hands, it is double reinforcement. Take the time to initiate conversations with people that you feel could use your services. There is really no excuse to not have clientele because there are many, many people in the world or better yet your town, that receive the services that you offer and there is no reason why they shouldn't be coming to you. You do not have to be insulting, just simply ask them where they get their hair, makeup, skin, waxing done and proceed from there.

If you are just out of school and are a new beauty advisor, go out and pass out cards while you are not busy in your salon or spa. Take a walk around the neighborhood and go to local businesses. Tell them the services that you offer and introduce yourself to people. Become a familiar face, and even if they are not coming to you now, they may begin coming to you in the future.

You never know, so developing relationships is key at this time.

Some new stylist and such feel as though they should not have to go out and do all of this. They feel like business will just come to them and show up at their door. I can assure you that this will not happen. Unless you are employed at an extremely busy salon or spa when you finally branch out on your own, the odds of business breaking down your door is slim to none. This is where your initiative should begin to kick in. This is not the time to be lazy, this is the time to kick things into full gear. Get up and get out there! This is the time to build.

When you are out there soliciting yourself for lack of better terms, be excited! No one wants an unenthusiastic, passionless person soliciting them. They want to see and feel your excitement. You may not want to be out there and would totally prefer to be inside but try your best to be as friendly an upbeat as possible. No one likes to do this part of the work but it is actually pretty effective.

Look good while you are out. Dress as professional as possible and speak as professionally as possible. I cannot stress how important this is. Whatever you are promoting, you should look the part. Hair should be clean and neat, makeup should be done and clothing should be clean and neat as well. If you are out looking disheveled and unruly, perspective clients will not trust that you have the skills they need to improve their look.

This is the time that you should begin to offer specials. If you are new to a salon or spa, most business owners do not mind offering specials to those that come in and book with you to promote name recognition. Although many people will ONLY come in because there is a deal or special offered, there are many people that will come in and enjoy what you have done for them and continue to book with you on a regular basis. This is an effective way to build new clientele whether you are new to the business or already existing as a business and looking to solicit new customers.

SOCIAL MEDIA MARKETING

This gets touchy. As it comes to social media marketing, this is the new craze and epidemic that has swept our nation. Whether young or mature, social media has become an effective way to reach out to old friends, stay in contact with family members not seen on a regular basis, promote your business and even solicit dates! As it comes to your business, it can be a very effective tool to promote, gain new clients, create a business entity, and reach out to perspective customers. An awesome entity if used properly.

This is where it can get tricky. You see, a long time ago, there was no such thing as social media. If a client wanted to get to know you, try your salon, make a complaint or etc. they had to come to your place of business. As of now, because of the dynamic of social media, clients can view your profile, see your personal life, take negative shots at your business, post complaints or even pictures. Good news can travel fast but bad news can travel even faster based on the likes of social media. If a client is dissatisfied, they can complain on MANY different sites and alert all of their friends and acquaintances as well. Clients can look you up and gain certain impressions of you based on your social media pictures, conversations, content and friends. You want to present yourself in the best light possible as a professional.

As a business professional, you should be very careful how you portray yourself on social media. This can go many ways. Clients gain certain impressions of you and if you are misrepresented or misunderstood it can affect your business negatively. Social media has even become a very popular way for employers to evaluate whether they will accept you as a part of their team. I obtained an interview for a position of salon manager, to my surprise I found out later that she had viewed my Facebook page before hiring me to get a feel of the kind of person I was and gain insight into my life. My Facebook page was private, but she was able to see my profile picture, as well as some basic information. She later told me, had she found anything that she didn't like or eluded to the fact that I might not be a good fit, she would not have hired me. Since that experience, I have seen many business owners go Facebook or Instagram stalking to see what their staff is portraying outside of work as well as if new prospects should be hired. This can only lead to the conclusion that...your social media representation is VERY IMPORTANT!

My advice for social media representation is simple.

- **Be very careful how you portray yourself on social media-** Some people do not realize how they are showcasing themselves on Facebook, Twitter, Instagram and any other network they participate in. Employers as well as potential clients are looking at your network and you want to represent yourself as accurately as possible. No one wants to see violence, explicit sexual references, or vulgar vocabulary. Beware of how you speak on social media about your private life and how you live it. Clients and employers want to know they are dealing with a professional, not an immature adult who showcases everything on their network, talks about others, gossips or slanders and thinks that the world is after them or "hating" on them so to speak. This is unbecoming and a turn off for both clients and employers. Take a look at your page from another point of view, and evaluate what it is that you are portraying. Every now and again, I take a look at my profile and scroll down my timeline, simply to see what the world may be seeing and I make adjustments if necessary based on the results that I want.

- **If you would like to use your pages for personal use-don't use it professionally or vice versa, pick one-** Your pages are what people will see when they look you up and it is perfectly okay to use your network for your personal use and private so that only friends and family may see. However, if you want to use it professionally, you should allot a separate profile for yourself professionally. This does not allow clients directly into your personal life and can keep your professional image intact.

When you have a professional page, you can promote specials, showcase your work, include client testimonials and communicate with clients. Your personal page should always be kept private and only accessible to those that are your friends and acquaintances. Try your best not to blur the lines. I have two business pages as well as a personal page, but I am still very reserved with the information that I put on my personal page as well. This helps me to keep my personal life and professional life separate.

- **Do not use it to talk about what you dislike about clients or your work-** This is very important! I have seen many times where individuals will put up something about their job or about a client in a general manner. Although you may not have named a client specifically, there is nothing to say that you were not talking about "them". This is what a client will think and feel. Do not talk about your job in a negative manner or your clients in a negative manner. This is super unprofessional. I have actually seen on Facebook where someone will make fun of a client's feet during a pedicure, post about their tragic Brazilian wax experience or make fun of a style choice that a client has made. This is for sure is a client base killer. Those that do come to you may be turned off and stop coming to you and those that do not come to you, may never come to you because of social networking behavior like this. Your job is to keep and build your client base, not to run away potential clients and existing clients because of immature behavior.

BE SELECTIVE

Once you have gotten the knack for networking whether in person or through social networking and have built yourself a small client base, be selective in who you target. This may sound contrary to what we have talked about earlier, but in the beginning your job is to target EVERYONE. You want to talk to everyone and solicit anyone to build yourself a base so that you can have a viable income, however, after some time you will need to be selective. All clients are not for everyone. You will find after some time that some clients are not a good fit for you and vice versa. Personality styles, personal preference, demeanor and the type of establishment you are in all play a very significant part in the type of clients that you will attract. Ask yourself, what type of client do you want to service? Do you want upscale clients, down to earth clients, fast paced clients, pampering clients? These are all very different types of customers and all of these will not be pleased in the same environment. What type of salon or spa do you work in? What type of clientele does it attract? These are important questions to ask because it will have an important role in the type of clients that you will attract as well. If you work in a fast paced salon focused on haircuts, it will be hard to get that luxurious woman who wants highlights and a sophisticated blow-dry every week. She will surely not fit into the fast paced environment. In a case like this, you will want to cater more to the school mom that may not have much time on her hands to get her haircut. Select your potential clients based on the environment that you can offer them. If you work in an upscale posh salon where the prices are expensive and you offer luxury services, you will want to cater more to the businesswoman who needs time off, time to pamper herself and relax and actually has the finances to pull it off. It is all about discerning who your best client base is, based on who you are and where you work.

Once you have cleared this up and have learned how to target specific clients, understand that there are certain clients that are not good for anyone to have to deal with. These clients will be the main reasons to make you want to quit, especially in the beginning if you receive a lot of these. We will discuss this group of people momentarily, but for now I want you to realize that these type of clients exist everywhere and affect everybody. The key is to not allow yourself to get discouraged especially if you are new to the business. I will list some of the clients below:

- **Never Satisfied Client-** This client is never satisfied with their hair, makeup, waxing, manicure or pedicure. No matter how great of a job you have done to them they will always want more. This client is never satisfied with themselves, so they will always exude this same energy outward. If you give a massage - they want a longer one, if you hand out free gifts – they want an extra one. This client will always find a reason to continue to come see you, yet they will not be satisfied completely when they leave. You will come to realize that this is just the type of person that they are, and in time it will no longer affect you.

- **Always Late Client-** This client is a super nuisance. They usually come charging in a hustle and bustle and they have 101 excuses for why they are running late and didn't get a chance to call. This client is always late and does not even call the desk or YOU to alert you that they are running behind. They are not considerate of your time, the fact that you will be running behind for your next client and they will still want their full service for the time allotted to them. This client is inconsiderate and although they are usually very likeable, they are bad for your business and will cause you a lot of stress on the day that they are scheduled to come in. How I have learned to handle these clients is to give them an appointment time that is at least fifteen minutes behind the time that I have given them, this relieves my stress and even if they happen to show up on time, which is rare, there is no harm done.

- **Wants a Miracle Client-** This client always comes in wanting to do the impossible. They have colored black hair and today they want to go back to blonde. This client brings in pictures of celebrities stating they want to look *exactly* like them. They have not done anything to their face in the past 30 years and today they want their facial to take off 30 years. This client can cause a small amount of stress because they want results that will take a miracle to deliver. Usually what they desire is not possible and cannot be achieved with one appointment, your best bet is to explain to this client that they will need to come back for several appointments to achieve what it is that they are looking for.

- **Never Has Enough Money Client-** This client comes in and realizes what it is that they need or you recommend to them what they need and at the end of the service they didn't realize that the cost was going to be over their budget. This client does not come in frequently hence the reason they never know the cost, but it can be frustrating cutting the cost of your service to accommodate them once the service was already completed. The easiest way to handle this, is to let your clients know up front what the cost of their service will be and let them determine whether they can afford it and continue from there. They may have to schedule a follow up appointment to get the rest of the service completed.

- **Wants a Hookup Client-**This client is usually a friend or a friend of a friend. This can get tricky because I am usually under the impression that clients are not our friends. They are familiar acquaintances. Friends that are our clients can become confusing and the lines can most definitely be blurred. The point here is this, you cannot do all of your friends and family's hair, makeup, skin, waxing, or nails for free. You may offer them a discount at your discretion but only at your discretion. There are some clients that hear about you based on your friends or acquaintances and they feel because they know your sister or friend that you will give them a significant discount or "hook up" You have to set your boundaries firmly and upfront in this case. There is a way to handle this professionally, when they call to book the appointment, educate them on your prices and let them know that the price will be determined after their consultation. This can erase any notion that you will not be charging them or knocking a big portion off of the price.

- **The Picky, Complaining Client-** This client is always going to find something to complain about or pick at after her service is complete.

This is the client after a blow-dry, or haircut that will pick up YOUR tools and begin to style their hair themselves in an effort to show you that it was not done to perfection or their liking. This client will complain that they were waiting too long even though you were only two minutes behind in taking them, they will complain that the salon or spa is too loud, they complain about kids in the waiting area, and other staff that you have no control over. They will always find small things to complain about along with the big things. They may complain about the hairstyle that you have given them even though it is what they specifically asked for. This client is a cause for much stress and this is the client that you DO NOT want! This client will never be satisfied and will end up complaining to all of her friends ultimately tainting your name, image and customer service. This client will come to you a few times and wind up leaving anyway. You will find that this client has hopped from salon to salon never to settle into one because she is never pleased. This client is the client that you would be much better off if she finds a new beauty consultant.

- **The Impatient Client-** This client is the client that is always in a rush. They don't have the time for the complete service and insists on rushing you throughout their service. They will want to shortchange service, walk out wet, take roller sets out before completely dry and stress you out about timing. They have too much on their plate and barely have time to get their services done although they desperately want

47

them and are in need of them. When you service this client, you will have to realize that they are always pressed for time and adjust your service times accordingly.

Recognize what you are good at and like to do and focus on attracting those clients.

THE VALUE OF TENTACLES

What are tentacles? Tentacles are a person that can reach a lot of people for you. This person has a network of people that they deal with themselves and if you get acquainted with this person it has the potential to do your business a world of good. Examples of tentacles would be; Restaurant Owners, Pastors, Doctors or Nurses, Group Leaders, Teachers, Retail Workers, Owners, & Managers. If you can get into contact with one of these types of clients, you have just connected yourself with an automatic network. These people are in constant proximity of other people and if you do a good job on any of their services, others will notice and inquire about them. These people also talk to others as a part of their job and may end up referring lots of people to you. When others are pleased with the work that you have done on them, they have no problem telling others what a great job you have done. If someone compliments them, they will automatically begin spewing the details of their service and who implemented it. This will be good news for you! Take advantage.

3

SELLING YOURSELF (Your Key to Success)

A huge part of building your beauty business is learning how to sell yourself. The reason behind this is because you are your business! If you do not have the skills to sell yourself and your services, no matter how good you are, no one will have the privilege of finding out. It's up to you to make yourself marketable as well as marketing yourself every opportunity you get. Marketing yourself is a very big aspect of this industry, without it, you have no business. Going to school and spending thousands of dollars for tuition only to graduate and become afraid to market yourself will undoubtedly cause you to become a failure in this business.

There are various ways to market yourself without being very aggressive about it, and these next helpful tips are a subtle but effective way to build your clientele.

LOOK THE PART

You are in the beauty industry, you should ALWAYS look the part! No exceptions! Your personal and professional image should reflect the beauty industry and your specific expertise. If you are an aesthetician, your skin should be taken care of to the best of your ability. If you are a stylist, your hair should be stylish and maintained at all times. If you are a makeup artist, your makeup should be done tastefully to compliment your outfit or event. You should always look and dress the part of the industry and there is no excuse to come out looking like you forgot all of your cosmetology teachings at home. It is very common to see hairdressers, makeup artists, barbers, and estheticians while out and their personal image does not reflect their industry at all. This is a very common way to miss opportunities to share your brand and your talent.

BE APPROACHABLE/ BE PERSONABLE

When out and about be approachable and converse with people. There are countless amount of times that I am at a local Beauty Supply store, the nail salon, Sally's or Cosmo and I strike up conversation and even give professional advice on products and hair care. This opens the door for me to suggestive sell my services or to hand out a business card. Being personable while out and about is the prime opportunity for you to let others know what you do and where you work. Offer smiles and openness, people like to talk to people that are friendly and approachable. This makes it easy for them to compliment you, ask you a question or inquire about services and products.

BECOME KNOWLEDGEABLE ABOUT YOUR CRAFT

You always want to be knowledgeable about your particular craft because knowledge is power. Why you ask? Knowledge creates confidence and confidence is key in this business. It is not a good position to be in when a client desires your expertise and you don't have a clue what they are talking about. You will surely lose confidence this way. The trick is to not only know *what* you are doing but know *why* you are doing it. Clients questions are usually based on the why not the what. Most clients will ask questions such as "Why does my hair not hold a curl"? "Why did you use liquid foundation instead of powder"? "Why does my skin breakout after I use this product"? They are usually focused on the *why*...keep this in mind. This is called the THEORY of what you are doing. In this business there are two facets, the practical, which is the practice of the art and the actual *doing,* as well as the theory which is the education behind what you are doing. There are many stylist, barbers, colorist, makeup artist and estheticians that are good in practical but they have no idea of the theory behind what they are doing. They merely have talented hands. What will set you apart and above the rest is to have the talent as well as the knowledge. This will cause you to become a very attractive force in this industry. Knowledge also helps you to gain your clients trust. This is important because once a client trusts you it causes them to continue to come back and buy "whatever" it is that you are selling. You may be selling products, services or your consulting services or classes, if a client trusts you it makes it easier for them to buy from you.

BE ARTICULATE

Clients need to be able to understand what it is that you are trying to communicate to them and where you are coming from. Usually when a client sits in your chair for the first time they are looking for you to answer their questions in a way that they are able to understand. Refrain from using technical words where a client may not have the slightest clue what you are referring to and keep slang to a minimum. There are technical words that we learn during schooling that can be left out of your consultation with a client. Once you have been seeing this client for a while, you still want to have professional communication with them because things can always be misconstrued and that is not something you want to happen in the long run. Another aspect that is very important is reflective communication. Reflective communication is repeating back to the client or customer what was just said in order to facilitate precise understanding. In this industry it is very common to have a misunderstanding because it is a creative industry. It is based on perceptions and what you see versus what I may see. A client may enter your business and during your consultation they may express that they want a hair color change. This client tells you they want red hair, in your mind you may see a reddish orange or true red and they may want a brownish red. This will be a huge cause for concern if you just go with what you *think* they meant versus what they truly meant. As it comes to hairdressing, makeup and even skin care it is very easy to misunderstand what a client truly wants based on miscommunication and perception this is why it is imperative to utilize the reflective listening.

BE EXCITED ABOUT YOURSELF AND WHAT YOU DO

This one is important and goes unnoticed quite frequently. It is very alluring to see someone excited about their craft, no one wants to be serviced by a tired stylist, esthetician, makeup artist etc. They want someone working on them that is passionate about what they do. Too many times customers are being serviced by beauty professionals that are tired, burnt out, unpassionate, and lack excitement. This will inadvertently cause clients to be attracted elsewhere. Clients can sense if you are no longer in love or excited about what you do, this is your career but unfortunately it is THEIR image that is at stake and compromised when you have no passion left in your soul for what you are doing. When you lack excitement about your craft, the client is the one that ends up suffering. Your creativity and talent does not flow as it should when you have lost your zest for the industry.

BE PROFESSIONAL

Professionalism goes a very long way in the industry and we will delve deeper into this subject in the next chapter, but for now there are a few key components that would be awesome career builders. As it comes to the beauty business, we have indeed become used to the flexibility and the fact that basically for lack of better terms we are our own boss. It takes a lot of responsibility to be your own boss especially if you are not quite ready for that responsibility. Most people have grown in the business world and have been selectively groomed before they become a boss or business owner, however in this industry because your business is you, you can come right out of school and begin to groom and grow your business immediately. This cause some to hit some severe hiccups in the early stages of their career because of the lack of business training.

Clients love to feel like they have something special and they love to feel as though they are important. They want to feel as though you enjoy servicing them and their business is important to you. It's your job to make them feel as such. There are a few keys ways to keep clients satisfied and continuing to utilize your services.

- BE ON TIME- Clients do not like waiting on their stylist, makeup artist, waxer, barber or anything else, they like to be serviced and they like to be serviced on time. It is a nuisance to have a scheduled appointment time only to be seen long after that time. Clients will become weary of the disrespect of their time and began to look elsewhere for their products and services.

- DON'T FUSS WITH CLIENTS- This is a big no no. No matter what mishaps may happen in the salon or spa atmosphere it is distasteful and unprofessional to go back and forth with a client over a misunderstanding. Be courteous, be professional and find the best way to deal with the situation while not losing a client in return. Remember bad news ALWAYS travels faster than good news and a disgruntled client can be a potential downfall to your business.

- BE ACCOMODATING- Clients love to feel as though you have gone the extra mile for them, even when in fact you may not have. It does not take a lot to offer your clients a service that makes them feel special. Accommodate their needs and wants if it is possible. Carry tea, water or coffee that you can offer them while they wait, try to accommodate small requests and give out rewards or gifts to loyal clients. If your client is loyal, don't hesitate to come in early or stay a little later to accommodate them. Gestures like this will go far in the long run.

- BE PROFESSIONAL IN COMMUNICATION-
  customers love to know that they are being
  serviced by a professional and your language is
  a big part of that role. It is your job to be
  respectful and courteous while a client is in your
  chair. They do not want to hear your swearing,
  arguments, phone conversations or problems at
  home. There may come a time when you have
  grown very close to a client and you begin to
  share personal stories but this is not a rule of
  thumb. You should always be as professional as
  possible when servicing your client. This is a
  huge part of building your clientele.

Selling yourself will be a huge part of building your
business. Until you can sell yourself effectively, clients
may never know about your talent, skills, passion or love
of this industry and how eager you are to serve them. If

you have trouble with this, give yourself a few goals to get yourself started. A good goal to have is to try to talk to at least three people a day about your products or services, after some time, people will begin to catch on. If you are nervous and have not yet mastered the art of talking to strangers and soliciting business, Facebook, Twitter and Instagram are wonderful tools to get your business on the map. Using these tools are very effective at advertising and promoting your business to people that you would have not met in your normal circle of influence. These tools enable you to become your own self marketer and assist you in building your business slowly but effectively.

4

<u>WHY CLIENTS DON'T COME BACK</u>

There are various reasons for losing clientele, and we will discuss a lot of them in the upcoming pages. I would like you to understand that clients usually want to stay loyal. It is a nuisance to continue to see different people for your hair, makeup or waxing if you do not have to. Clients get comfortable with who they see and once they attain that comfort ability they are usually around for the long haul. Can you imagine getting your hair colored and having to tell a new stylist every time you go into the salon what you would like it to be and what you do not want it to be? This can be nerve wrecking! Or better yet you receive Brazilian waxes and you go to a new spa every single time and have to tell the esthetician what to do to make you feel comfortable.

This would not be fun and clients would usually rather not see someone new after they have grown comfortable with a certain beauty specialist. All of this being said, there are some very key reasons why a client would inconvenience themselves and begin to see someone new. These reasons may or may not cause a loyal client to leave but if they do leave I can almost guarantee you it will fall into one of these reasons.

BAD LOCATION- This is important. There are many different reasons for why a location would be considered bad. Clients can be really picky about the location in which they are serviced.

- **No Parking-** This will cause clients much frustration as they are coming to get serviced. It is essential that you either open an establishment or attain employment at an establishment that has ample parking for your customers. Clients will began to grow weary of parking around the corner or far away from the establishment. This is something to take a look at when seeking to attain employment or looking for rental space.

- **Too Much Going On/ Loitering/ Sales-** Clients do not like coming to a place of business that has too much going on in or near the place of business. There should not be people allowed to hang outside the door of your business, or people allowed to solicit during business. This can be quite a nuisance for those getting serviced. They are here to relax and get away, not to be solicited with sales from someone off the street. Clients will also quite frequently become uncomfortable with loiterers and people especially men hanging outside the door of your business. Even if your business is in a common area like a mall or plaza, it is your responsibility to make sure that no one loiters near the door of your establishment.

- **Parking Meters/ Paid Parking-** This will always be a deterrent for clients. They already have to pay for their services from you and now they have to pay for parking as well which makes their overall expense for you very pricey. This will become cause for clients to start shopping elsewhere to save a little bit of money for themselves. Paid parking can become expensive especially if clients come in and get services that take quite some time to complete. If at all possible, try to stay away from business that make clients pay for parking, this will always lessen the clientele you can attract.

- **Bad Neighborhood-** Let's face it, there are some neighborhoods that are a little worse than others and it would be best to stay away from those neighborhoods when seeking to grow your business. Clients may follow you anywhere but when the neighborhood is not good they may weigh the reward against the risk and end up leaving you. No one wants to come outside and risk getting robbed or harassed on their way to their car especially at night. Try to work at a place that has good lighting in the parking lot or possibly cameras to deter criminals from hanging around your place of business.

DISSATISFIED WITH SERVICE- There can be many reasons as to why a client can be dissatisfied with the service rendered. This will be one of the biggest reasons that a client will not continue to see you for their beauty needs. There are various ways to cause a client to be unhappy with the services that you offered and I will list some of them below.

- **Lack of Skill-** Clients are coming to you as a professional to receive a professional level of service. If you are not good at something or do not possess a certain level of skill with something do not attempt to try them out on a client. You may need to take more classes, education and receive more training before you embark on offering a certain service that you are not quite polished with yet. There are certain procedures that I will not do because I am not the best at it. I refuse to do perms and certain methods of hair color, these are not my expertise. If someone comes to me requesting those types of services I will not hesitate to refer them to someone that does perform at that expert level. This is not a reflection of your professional ability, it simply means that you would prefer for them to see a colleague rather than risk their dissatisfaction with you. Clients respect if you do not try to perform a service that you are not great at. They would much rather you opt out of doing the service then to attempt it and they are not satisfied.

- **Mediocre Results-** Mediocre results will result in client loss and they will only give a few tries before finally trying someone else to get the results that they want. Mediocre results are when a client is not completely dissatisfied with the service but they feel it could be or look a little better. This can stem from lack of skill, distractions, rushing, lack of passion, and the list goes on and on. The reason is not relevant, however what is relevant is that it will be the cause of customer breakdown. These clients will eventually make their way to another beauty specialist if the mediocrity keeps up.

- **Didn't Get What They Asked For-** This is no good because clients are coming to see you for certain results. They are expecting you as the professional to deliver the results that they want. They may come in with pictures from a magazine or pictures of themselves requesting something specific. It is up to you to grant this request. If you cannot grant it, it is up to you to communicate this. Otherwise, you will find yourself in a situation where your client is left with a service they are truly not happy with. This can boil down to a key components. Communication, if you and your client do not communicate effectively about what the client requires, this can lead to a huge misunderstanding that can become a catastrophe.

- **Mistake Made-** This can happen to even the most seasoned of professionals. A bang is cut to short, a person is burned by wax, a color is brassy and cannot be toned, a haircut is cut too short etc. This is okay, but you most definitely run the risk of losing this client. If this is your first time servicing them the odds are about 95% that they will not be returning to you, if you have serviced this client before they may take a risk and come to see you again. Understand when it is your first time servicing a customer, you only get ONE chance to make a first impression, make it count! This is your time to shine and let them know they need your services.

- **Untimely Service-** In a nutshell, this means that their service took entirely too long. Clients do not want to spend their entire day getting a service no matter how great that service may be. They are giving you their time and they are expecting for you to respect it. Do not schedule someone a 9:30 appointment and then finally get to see them at 11am, this will be a sure cause for a disgruntled customer and as much as they may love the way that you service them, eventually they will get fed up at the lack of regard for their time and go elsewhere.

There are so many reasons that a client would leave and not come back and continue to receive your services, more reasons than you can count, but the above listed reasons are the most prevalent and the most common. Clients would prefer to stay loyal but if you exhibit any of the behaviors or tendencies listed above I can assure you that your client base will be short lived. This is a sure way to lose existing clients as well as deter potential clients from coming to your place of business. Remain professional and your business will flourish!

5

UNPROFESSIONALISM (Your Business Killer)

Unprofessionalism is the BIGGEST catalyst for failing your business. Although in the grand scheme of things it seems small, it is actually the biggest tactic that you can have to build and *keep* your clientele. It is one thing to service a lot of people, it's another thing entirely to keep those clients year after year, service after service. Studies show that 20% of the service is skill and the other 80% is customer service. This is a customer related business and if you do not have great customer service you have lost the game before you even started. Customer service is the pillar of your business whether you realize it or not. Customers love when they come to an establishment and they feel wanted when they come in, they love to feel special and as though their patronage is truly appreciated. Have you ever been to a certain place of business and were not greeted when you walked into the door? Or better yet, have you been checking out and not told thank you on your way out? These are surefire ways to urge a client not to return. I am very picky about where I spend my money and when I support your business I want to be appreciated so I offer that same appreciation in return. This is what clients require, it is a non-negotiable.

This customer service starts from the desk to the chair. This means that client should feel welcome from the MOMENT that they walk into the door. If your front desk staff is not on point, you have lost the battle before you even started. Your front desk staff is the first person that a client sees before he or she gets to you. This staff should always be on point. They should be dressed nicely, well- spoken and very friendly.

When a client walks in, they should be greeted with a smile and an immediate "Hello". This shows that you recognize them upon arrival. This is important. Your front desk staff is one of the most important entities of the business. They can make or break your business in a very big way. If a client comes in and feels disrespected or insulted before they even get to you, no matter how great your ability is, the service and their overall experience has been compromised. Most people do not realize how important first impressions are, within the first ten minutes of entering an establishment a client has already gauged their perspective on the place. If your front desk staff is rude, ornery, incompetent and unaccommodating it will affect your business in an adverse way.

Timing is a big deal in this industry, and clients detest when you are late for their appointment. This shows a lack of respect and a disregard for their time. Anything after seven minutes they start counting the time. Clients will give five to ten minutes as a grace period but anything after that time frame, they will begin to get frustrated. This can be an easy fix, it truly boils down to lack of time management and booking correctly. You should always book for the time of service that is being rendered. For instance, if a haircut takes you thirty minutes, book thirty minutes for the service and book your next client accordingly. If you are running behind, call your next client and alert them that there may possibly be a small wait. This allows them to prepare for the wait and they still feel as though their time was respected. Take responsibility for your booking, realize that once you are running behind for one client, the time only accumulates by the end of your day. If you were only ten minutes behind for your first client, by the end of the day you may be thirty minutes behind for your last client unless you find a way to catch up. Customers also do not like if you take too long for their service in general. A haircut should not take an hour and a half and they are not expecting it to. If you continue taking long time periods to do simple services, you will lose your client base and also end up losing money this way. I work at a spa and it takes me all of 15-20 minutes to do a full Brazilian wax, some therapist take an hour. However, most clients end up requesting me simply because I can get them in and out and they don't have to suffer through the long wait. I can also maximize my income this way. The longer it takes you to do a service, the less money that you make.

Unprofessional conversations can be a huge turn off for some clients. This can consist of many things but to name a few are gossiping about other clients or staff.

This can cause clients to think that you do the same towards them when they are not around. It is unbecoming and unprofessional to talk about other's personal affairs in your place of business. Some clients may love it, but the professional clients that you would want to support your business will not take lightly to it. Debating about religion or politics is another very touchy subject to talk about in a business setting. Another topic to beware and use caution when bringing up is race and stereotypes. It can rev people up and cause them to become emotional and angry when defending their views. These are topics that I would steer clear of when servicing clients.

Inappropriate language and too much detail about your night etc. leave these conversations for your friends. Don't get me wrong, clients love to hear good stories but when you start talking over their heads to other stylists, going into extreme detail about what happened during your night out on the town, talking and laughing loudly, these can all be a turn off for your more reserved clients. This leads me to the act of degrading other stylists or salons while at work. It is very unprofessional to talk about other members of the staff to your clients. This is distasteful and shows a lack of respect, not good qualities to showcase to a person that you wish to remain loyal to you. It is also not a good idea to talk negatively about other salons to your clients. You never know who people may know and word travels fast. You do not want to gain the reputation of being negative or a gossip, it is unbecoming and will cause people to stay away from you and become leery of receiving your services.

Clients look at everything, they are very observant and will judge your place of business based on the way it looks. It is of upmost importance to have clean and tidy work stations. It is gross to have dirty stations and dirty work areas. This is a huge turn off for a client and they will never want to come back if they think that you are unsanitary. Always be sure to clean up after each client. State law says that hair should be swept up within three minutes of your client being completed. Make sure that you sanitize your implements. Combs, brushes, makeup brushes, blades, tweezers etc. should all be sanitized in a hospital grade solution when your service is completed. Clients will take a look at the salon, spa, barbershop as well. Your station may be clean but if the overall establishment is dirty, clients WILL notice. If it is *your* establishment and you just don't have the time to clean it, hire a cleaning person to come in maybe once or twice a week to help you maintain the place, if it is not your place of business meaning you don't own it, and don't have jurisdiction over how the business looks, it is your job to call a meeting with the owner or possibly find a new place of employment. Working in a dirty, untidy establishment will hurt your business and your client growth in a very big way.

A beauty business, no matter what it is, should have structure. There should be an order of how things are run. There should always be a front desk staff, however if your place of business does not have that luxury, stylists should greet every client as they walk through the door. Front desk staff/ Salon/Spa Coordinators are great because they help the business run more efficiently. They run the appointment book, answer questions and phone calls, collect payment, sell products, greet clients when you are busy and maintain the cleanliness of the front. If there is no structure, clients may get lost in the shuffle of the hustle and bustle of things going on. When there is no order or structure, clients feel lost and shuffled around. This is not comfortable and causes them to become apprehensive about returning. There are some business that may even allow children to be involved. If your business allows children make sure they are in a designated area. Children should not be allowed to run in and or around the salon. This is super unprofessional and not to mention annoying. I have children myself and God knows I love them but most people come to the salon or spa to get a break from their children not to help take care of other's children. Children are sweet and cute, but this is a different scenario when they are disturbing others' peace.

Clients should always know when, where and who to pay. This is very uncomfortable for the client to have their service completed and then have to ask someone who or where to pay. This should be structured and set up previously and explained to the client upon arrival or posted somewhere that can be readily seen.

As it comes to professionalism, your professional image is what will be the catalyst of attraction for you. It is not okay to look unprofessional in your appearance when you work in the beauty industry. It's actually absurd! How are you going to be a walking advertisement if you yourself look like a train wreck? I hate to be so candid but it is the truth. You cannot expect people to believe that you can take them to another level when you look like you have not made it to that level yourself. This is about BUSINESS, not your personal preference. I know, it feels wonderful to walk around in a yoga pants with a freshly washed face but that is not attracting anybody to you for business. I make it a point, whether going to the gym or to the grocery store to always look and feel my best. Why? Because I am my best advertisement. I cannot tell you how many clients I have gained from going to the gym and my hair actually looked nice and was not pulled into a messy ponytail. I have had people compliment my skin and my hair while working out! When I am at the grocery store, I receive compliments on the natural look of my makeup and have given tutorials to complete strangers that I met while out. I always have a business card available and I use every opportunity to promote myself and my business. There is no excuse to have on pajama pants while out in public… it is not acceptable, no exceptions! It is also not okay to walk around in hair bonnets and headscarves while out in public or at work. I understand and have even done it myself, you finally get the time to do your own hair and a client walks in and wants to be serviced, this is perfectly okay, but when this is your normal and you walk around like this as a rule of thumb, I can't tell you how detrimental this will be to building your business. You absolutely have to look the part in order to convince others that you can help them look the part. I a very selective about who I let do my services. I normally do them myself but in rare occasions when I need someone else to do them, I am very selective with whom I choose. I will never allow someone who does not ever wear makeup or I've never seen them in makeup, apply my makeup. It's that simple. If your hair is never done, I will never trust you to style or color mines. I cannot count the endless amount of times that I have seen a fellow stylist at the mall or at the store and I am embarrassed for them based on their appearance. The funny thing is, this person is always making excuses for their appearance. Apologizing for how they look and explaining how they just ran out for a second to grab something. I make sure that I am never in that position where I have to explain to others how I look when they catch me at my random moments. This is just the price I have to pay for being in this industry. It is actually not that big of a price, it does not cost you much to throw on a dab of makeup and do something to you hair before you step outside the house. This is the small price you have to pay to become attractive enough to be able to freely talk about your business and what you have to offer. Take my word for it, you will receive clients in this inadvertent way without even actively trying.

Unprofessionalism is the biggest business killer for many beauty businesses. It is a common belief that just because you are in the beauty industry, you do not have to be as professional as you would if you work at a bank or a corporate office and this may be true, but professionalism is required even in this business if you want it to last. The biggest complaint that I hear now, as I teach, is that clients wants consistency, reliability, and professionalism.

Clients are the biggest part of your business, and without them your business will be short lived. It is our jobs as professionals to keep them happy and loyal to us. This does not take much effort on our part but it does take *some* effort on our parts. I can assure you that if you use the tips and techniques listed in this book you will grow your business and take it to another level. The information listed is simple and easy and will only take a moment to modify in your own personal business. Take the time to modify some of your business and marketing tactics and watch your business grow like it has never grown before. It is usually the simple things that need modification and once these are taken care of, you will begin to soar!

Take the time to evaluate your business and where it is at physically and financially. Do you need more clients to maintain? Would you like to expand your business/employees? This is the time to take inventory of where you are and where you want to be? Upgrade your image and upgrade the image of your business.

Build Your Business Fast!

These two components alone will assist you in attracting more clients and new people your way.

I hope you have enjoyed the information given in this book. It is wise to seek a professional in business consulting to bring your business to reach new heights. This works wonders for growing your business. My information is listed at the bottom of this page should you need additional help.

Tonisha Dawson

Osunallurebeauty@gmail.com

Osunallureacademy.com

Tonishadawson.com

Osunallurehmboutique.com

Build Your Business Fast!

Printed in Great Britain
by Amazon